Three Australian Plays

Peter Levy

Copyright @ 2020
Peter Levy
All rights reserved

ISBN: 978-0-6485152-9-6

This publication may not be reproduced, stored in a retrieval system, or transmitted in whole or in part, in any form or by any means, electronically, mechanically, photocopying, recording, or otherwise without the direct consent of the author.

Published in Australia
Printed by Ingram Spark

Three Australian Plays

Author: Peter Levy
peter@peterlevy.com.au
61403604213

Prior works:
System Error: The Diary of My Reconfiguration
Betsy Collins
Knowing Touch

Contents

TWO FUCKIN' HOURS   1

NATURE OF THE BEAST   19

THE COFFIN   66

TWO FUCKIN' HOURS

by

Peter Levy

Copyright 2020

1. Ext CITY STREET LATE NIGHT ... 1 HOUR LATER

Charles, Robert and Amy, are homeless people camped under a street light in the city.

A thug goes directly over to Charles in a most provocative manner.

THUG 1
You think you're so tough, do ya?

CHARLES
I don't want any fuckin' trouble! Can't you see we have enough already?

THUG 1
Just what I though! You're a yellow cunt!

ROBERT
(pleading)
Leave us alone.

THUG 2
(yelling to his mate)
Give it to 'em!

Thug 1 throws a punch at Charles who ducks away from it only to be charged at by the thug who pounces on him kicking and trying to elbow Charles as he goes.

Charles goes from a defensive mode to one on the attack but the thug is too strong and fast for him and they are soon locked in a battle where the thug has Charles in a headlock that is choking him.

THUG 1
(to Charles)
You're fuckin' already dead! You just don't know it yet!

The thug pulls out a shiny hunting knife and slips it into Charles. Blood spurts everywhere.

CHARLES
(gasping for breath)
Fucking Bastard ...

Charles collapses and dies as the thug turns his attention to Robert and Amy. Robert's dog, Elvis, goes for the thug and one of the other thugs pulls out a gun and shoots it dead. Robert is terrified and frozen to the spot. Amy screams for help.

AMY
(screaming)
Help! Fucking hell, somebody help us!

Thug 1 wipes his knife on dead Charles' body and turns to Amy

THUG 1
Shut the fuck up, bitch!

The thug then whacks her across the face with the butt of his knife and rips her shirt off exposing her bra. Blood trickles down her face. The thug then goes and punches her into her eye and Amy is totally dazed.

THUG 1
(ripping off her bra)
Let's see what you got, bitch!

AMY
(bruised and confused)
What's happening to me?

THUG 2
(smirking while he holds Amy down)
You're getting a real man now!

Thug 1 rips off her dress and undies, releases his own belt so that his pants drop to the ground, pulls down his boxers and jumps onto her.

                              THUG 1
                            (violently)
                    Move and I'll fuckin' kill you!

Amy nods and looks over to Robert who is whimpering over his dog. Two other thugs, pull out knives and look menacingly at Robert, while they wait their turn with Amy.

                              THUG 1
                    You're fuckin' dry as all shit!

Thug 1 wipes his hand over Amy's face where she is bleeding profusely and rubs it into her vagina.

                              THUG 1
                        (smiling as he rapes her)
                   Ah! That's better! That's a good girl!

The three other thugs circle the rape chanting

                         3 THUGS TOGETHER
                      Give it to her! Give it to her!

After Thug 1 has had his pleasure, the other three thugs take it in turn to pounce on Amy and rape her as well.

Some passer-bys see what is taking place and scurry off. One rings the police and another tries to video it on his mobile phone.

                              THUG 3
                           (glaring at them)
                   We're only cleaning up the city! Fuck off!

The onlookers scurry away and the four thugs leave Amy on the ground bleeding all over as they run off into the shadows.

                           END OF SCENE 1

2. EXT CITY STREET LATE NIGHT - PRESENT TIME

Amy stops by a homeless man, Charles, and asks for help.

AMY
(tearfully to Charles)
Can I sleep here for the night? I won't be any trouble. I'm scared and tired. Please!

CHARLES
(groughly)
I'm not running a fuckin' hotel you know.

AMY
I know. I'm exhausted. Please.

CHARLES
(softening a little)
Just don't annoy me. Find another place tomorrow. Ok?

AMY
Mmm.

Some people pass by ... some drop coins ... most don't.

Another man, Robert, and his dog, Elvis, stop and Robert speaks to Charles.

ROBERT
I'm bunking here. Ok with you?

CHARLES
Have I got a fuckin' sign up or something?

ROBERT
I need to bunk down for the night. No trouble!

CHARLES
(chatting roughly to Robert)
If you think you can just take over our spot then bloody think again!

ROBERT
You don't own the street and I'll go where I want to, that's for sure.

CHARLES
Well sleep some place else then!

AMY
I don't need this!

CHARLES
(to Amy)
You bloody stay out of this!

ROBERT
(slowly)
What about one night, you bastard. I'll go in the morning. I promise.

CHARLES
One night?

ROBERT
Yeah, I swear! The cunts down there stole my bench. There were three of them coppers with fuckin' truncheons. I won't be trouble. I swear!

CHARLES
I've seen you before ...

ROBERT
I seen you too. Cops got it in for me is all.

CHARLES
You still pushing?

ROBERT
(calming down a bit)
Shit no! Broke! Can you spare a few bucks?

CHARLES
(harshly)
Fuck no! What do you think I'm loaded or something?

ROBERT
I had to ask. Thanks for the spot.

Charles just grunts at Robert and they both look at Jason as he passes them by. They are used to people doing that but he appeared to be watching them. They take more notice when he returns to them.
They all glance over at Jason who has made his way back to the group to just stand there without saying anything.

CHARLES
(a little aggressively)
What's on your mind Buster!

Robert's dog, Elvis, gets up and snarls at Jason.

JASON
(tentatively)
Will he bite me?

ROBERT
Depends.

Jason appears a little uncertain as to what to say next.

ROBERT (CONT'D)
(lightening up a bit)
What do ya want?

JASON
(a little relieved)
Looking for my daughter is all.

ROBERT
(looking in Amy's direction)
He your dad?

AMY
My dad's in Queensland.

JASON
I'm her step-dad. Amy, your mum's worried sick and so am I. Please come back home with me.

AMY
(yelling)
Not on your fucking life! I'm never going back!

JASON
It'll be different …

AMY
Sure! You're a fucking paedophile!

CHARLES
(looking angrily at Jason)
That true?

Jason doesn't say anything. Just glares at Amy.

CHARLES
I can tell! You're the lowest cunt around! Fuck off!

Jason moves off into the shadows. Still lurking around not sure what to do next.

People are always walking by without looking over or stopping. An elderly couple walking hand in hand stops briefly and the man pulls out a swag of coins and places them in the empty box.

CHARLES
(looking up at them)
Thanks, much appreciated.

OLD MAN
You're welcome. Sorry it's not more.

The old couple walk off. Two Policemen walk by and Jason flags them down.

JASON
Officers, my step daughter, Amy, is over there with those two guys. Is there anything you can do so I can take her home safely.

POLICEMAN
We're on a job right now but I'll chat to her if you like.

JASON
That would be great. Thanks.

The Policemen go over to Charles, Amy and Robert.

POLICEMAN
(to Amy)
Are you Amy? Don't you think you'd be better off at home?

AMY
I'm much better here, believe me!

POLICEMAN
I've got your father here

AMY
He's my bloody step-father and he's the bloody problem!

POLICEMAN
(taking an interest)
What do you mean?

AMY

My parents split up a couple of years ago. Dad went off to Queensland and my Mum hooked up with him.

POLICEMAN
And?

AMY
He started coming into my room at night. I told my mum and she didn't believe me. It kept happening night after night and so one day after school I just didn't come home.

POLICEMAN
Did you go to friends?

AMY
Tried that but it didn't work out that well either.

POLICEMAN
What about your church?

AMY
None of that stuff. I just stumbled onto these guys and that was that. At least I'm sort of safe here.

POLICEMAN
(taking out his pad and pen)
All right, I've made a note about it and I'll phone it in too. We'll be back soon. Ok?

AMY
I guess so.

The Policemen see Robert and his dog sitting there too.

POLICEMAN
(to Robert)
I've already told you once tonight to piss off from here didn't I? You better be gone by the time we get back! I've got no time for druggies!

The Policemen march off just as four thugs, who have been obviously drinking a bit stroll by. One of them pulls out three five cent coins and throws them into the coin box.

THUG 1
(laughing)
Knock yourselves out!

CHARLES
(getting annoyed)

Thanks mate!

THUG 2
It's all you're worth! You're all scum-buckets!

CHARLES
And you're just an arsehole!

The thug and his cohorts stop in their tracks and glare at the group. Seeing Amy, they address their next attention to her.

THUG 1
Hey sweetie, want to have a good time tonight?

ROBERT
(interjecting)
She's fine right where she is guys. Leave us alone, will you?

THUG 1
(angrily)
Wasn't talking to you!

By this time Elvis gets up menacingly looking at the four men and snarling.

CHARLES
(getting up)
Well I'm talking to you, so piss off!

AMY
(getting upset)
I'm not going anywhere. Especially not with you!

One of the thug spits at the group and then walks off.

THUG 2
(calling out)
Losers! Bloody losers!

Charles consoles Amy and winks at Robert

CHARLES
(reflectively)
But at least we're not arseholes!

They laugh, but in their laugh there's fear of what might happen next time.

Jason comes out of the shadows and approaches the thugs. Parked nearby in the darkness is a Salvation Army van with a lady in the front seat. She is unseen by Jason and the thugs.

JASON
(to the thugs)
Want to earn some easy money?

THUG 1
Doing what?

JASON
My daughter over there won't come home. I reckon if you could rough up the other two ...

THUG 1
What's in it for us then?

JASON
Two hundred do it?

THUG 1
Four hundred is cleaner. A hundred each.

JASON
(pulling out the notes from his wallet)
Ok. Do it quickly will you?

THUG 1
A half hour. They got a dog. Got a gun in the car, see.

JASON
(getting a bit concerned)
Just don't hurt the girl, ok?

THUG 1
Sure. Leave it to us.

The thugs wander off and Jason follows them for a bit and then returns to a spot under a street light.

He pulls out his mobile phone and calls his wife, Kerry, mother to Amy.
SPLIT SCREEN STYLE ... JASON & KERRY SPEAKING VIA THE MOBILE PHONE

JASON
Is that you Kerry?

KERRY

(upset)
Did you find her?

JASON
Yes, I found her.

KERRY
Thank God! You're a good man, Jason.

JASON
She's with some bums and addicts I'm afraid.

KERRY
She alright?

JASON
At the moment.

KERRY
Can't you get her to come back home?

JASON
She won't talk to me.

KERRY
Why?

JASON
I don't know. You better come down here and talk to her yourself.

KERRY
Alright love, text me the address and I'll come straight away.

JASON
(texting into his phone as he speaks)
Doing it now. Hurry!

KERRY
I will. 'Bye!

Jason wanders out of view towards where the thugs went off to.

An old codger swaggers past and is itching to get in on some conversation with them or anyone. He puts a coin in their box.

OLD CODGER
Just like after the war.

CHARLES
Thanks mate. It's still a bloody war.

OLD CODGER
I guess it is.

ROBERT
Got a smoke, mate?

OLD CODGER
(giving a couple of cigarettes to Robert)
Sure. Got a food voucher too. You could do more with it than me I reckon.
See you later.

ROBERT
yeah, Thanks.

OLD CODGER
(waving an arm in the air)
It's nothing.

The old codger swaggers off, watched by Charles and Robert.

AMY
He seemed like a nice enough bloke to me

CHARLES
You still have a lot to learn about people. They are not always what they seem.

A well-dressed man in a suit and tie wanders into their space and stands in front of Charles.

CHARLES
(quite casually)
So what's your game, mate? What barrow are you pushing?

The well-dressed man eyes off Elvis and then resumes a fixed gaze on Charles.

WELL-DRESSED MAN
(looking very sure of himself)
Nothing.

CHARLES
(getting a little annoyed)

Well piss off then!

WELL-DRESSED MAN
(dropping a coin in the box)
You don't have to talk to me like that ...

CHARLES
(interrupting him)
Sure. Don't need your fucking high and mighty round here. Just piss off!

The Well Dressed Man saunters off as the four thugs wander back to where the trio of homeless people are chatting. They are totally taken by surprise to see the thugs again so soon.

Thug 1 goes directly over to Charles in a most provocative manner, they are soon on the ground fighting. Jason is watching on from the shadows.

THUG 1
(to Charles)
You're fuckin' already dead! You just don't know it yet!

The thug pulls out a shiny hunting knife and slips it into Charles. Blood spurts everywhere.

CHARLES
(gasping for breath)
Fucking Bastard ...

Charles collapses and dies as the thug turns his attention to Robert and Amy. Robert's dog, Elvis, goes for the thug and one of the other thugs pulls out a gun and shoots it dead. Robert is terrified and frozen to the spot. Amy screams for help.

AMY
(screaming)
Help! Fucking hell, somebody help us!

Thug 1 wipes his knife on dead Charles' body and turns to Amy

THUG 1
Shut the fuck up, bitch!

The thug then whacks her across the face with the butt of his knife and rips her shirt off, exposing her bra. Blood trickles down her face. The thug then goes and punches her into her eye and Amy is dazed. She is then raped by the four thugs.

The onlookers scurry away and the four thugs leave Amy on the ground bleeding as they run off in Jason's direction. Jason is terrified but confronts them.

JASON
(nervously)
Why did you have to do that?

THUG 1
(laughing)
You want to be next?

Jason backs off in terror as the thugs leave.

The Salvation Army van, going from position to position delivering food, moves around the corner and is parked right across where the rape occurs.

Amy is dazed, bruised and bloodied. Robert is a total mess trying to console her and himself. Charles is lying dead. A Salvation Army lady in uniform sees the unfortunate scene and takes off her jacket to put around Amy.

SALVATION ARMY LADY
(sympathetically to Amy)
Let me get you to a hospital, dear.

AMY
(dazed and confused)
Where am I?

SALVATION ARMY LADY
(comfortingly)
You're safe now. I am here for you.

AMY
(screaming)
I want my mum! I just want my mum!

The two policemen walk back

POLICEMAN
(forcefully to Robert)

I told you to go! Move along!

Robert looks at them with pleading eyes but can say nothing as the trauma has him completely frozen.

SALVATION ARMY LADY
(sternly)
And where do you suggest he goes then?

POLICEMAN
He's a drug pusher! Lowest of the lows!

SALVATION ARMY LADY
What about this poor girl, officer?

POLICEMAN
She would be better off going home I'd say. Wouldn't you?

SALVATION ARMY LADY
(speaking very slowly)
I don't think so.

POLICEMAN
(turning to Robert)
It's move or I'm arresting all of you. What's it to be?

With a look of resignation, Robert looks at Amy and starts gathering up his things. The Salvation Army Lady helps Amy to her feet.

POLICEMAN (CONT'D)
If I see you again I'll arrest you!

ROBERT
(dropping Elvis to the ground)
Come on mate. I'm bloody going. That's enough isn't it?

POLICEMAN
Just get going before I change my mind!

Robert starts to slowly move away, but stops to gather up Charles' sleeping bag and a few other items, including the box with a few coins still in it.

The Salvation Army Lady looks back at the policeman and says.

SALVATION ARMY LADY
(angrily)

Satisfied now are you?

POLICEMAN
(Smiling nastily)
Just doing my job. Just cleaning up the city.

Kerry and Jason rush in from the shadows. Kerry grabs Amy from the Salvation Army Lady.

KERRY
(angry and teary)
Come here baby! Oh my God, what have they done to you?

AMY
(still in a daze)
Is that you Mum?

KERRY
Yes dear. I'm taking you home. Whatever it is, we can work it all out at home.

AMY
(crying)
Mummy!

KERRY
I'm here baby! I'm here!

The Salvation Army Woman looks angrily at Jason and then faces Kerry.

SALVATION ARMY LADY
Lady, this girl needs a hospital. She's been raped!

KERRY
(angry and teary)
Oh my sweet Jesus! No!

SALVATION ARMY LADY
Let me help you.

KERRY
How did this happen?

Jason shrugs his shoulders

SALVATION ARMY LADY
(angrily pointing a finger at Jason)
I know! Ask him!

KERRY
What do you mean?

SALVATION ARMY LADY
He didn't see me, but I was in the van when I saw him hand money to the thugs that did this to your daughter.

JASON
(protesting)
She's speaking garbage! I came here to find her!

SALVATION ARMY LADY
(staring at Jason)
So what were you doing with those lowlifes? You were up to no good weren't you?

KERRY
(looking up at Jason)
Is that true?

JASON
Of course not!

Amy lifts her head and scowls at Jason.

AMY
(looking back up at her mother)
You never bloody believed **me**, did you?

Scene 1 Charles is knifed to death and Amy assaulted and raped.

Scene 2 introduces the 4 characters and sees Jason trying to lure Amy to go back home. Some thug throws three 5cent coins into their money box and taunts them with jeering. Rough words are spoken and Charles is pissed off by it. Jason pays the thugs to come back and rough Robert & Charles up so that he can take Amy away from them back home. Amy's mum, Kerry, joins in for the finale.

AMY
Young girl around 16 years old, long unkempt hair, blue jeans with holes in them, a torn sweater and a beanie. Dirty and scrawny in appearance.
backstory: Mother remarried after a nasty divorce, father disappeared into a new relationship, stepfather started looking at Amy with lustful intentions, Amy tells her mother who refuses to believe it, Amy hits the streets.

CHARLES
Unshaven, in his late thirties, wearing an old blue pinstriped suit and what was once a white shirt that has definitely seen better days. Shoes are well worn and no socks. Used to be an accountant and then became a stockbroker. Lost everything virtually overnight due to some bad decisions and found himself on the street without a clue as to how to get back to his old life.

JASON
Early fifties, wearing a plain suit and tie. Medium height and build. A paedophile and step-daughter to Amy.

ROBERT
Late thirties, lean and mean, wearing old jeans, a sweater, a dark green hoody and beaten-up runners. A drug user and pusher on the street with his dog, Elvis, as his only protection and companion.

WELL DRESSED MAN
Late forties. A wanker.

SALVATION ARMY LADY
Late thirties in full attire.

POLICEMEN
Early thirties in uniform.

NATURE OF THE BEAST

by

Peter Levy

© 2020

SCENE 1

1. INSIDE A DOCTOR'S OFFICE

An ever present memory of several action scenes showing a soldier killing villagers during the Vietnam War, hovers over the head of Fred Martin, 70s, while he is having a first consultation with his local GP, Dr Rachel Solomon. He is annoyed and irritable while she is trying to remain calm and cool. She gets a temperature gun and aims it at his forehead.

FRED MARTIN
(annoyed)
I just had that fuckin' test when I got to the clinic!

DR RACHEL SOLOMON
(gloved and masked up)
That's right. Can't be too careful. You appear ok.

FRED MARTIN
(smugly)
From five minutes ago? Of course I'm bloody ok!

DR RACHEL SOLOMON
I haven't seen you before. Are you new to the area?

FRED MARTIN

I don't go to fuckin' doctors. Lived around here all my miserable life.

DR RACHEL SOLOMON

These are strange times alright.

FRED MARTIN

Not bloody telling me anything.

DR RACHEL SOLOMON

What can I do for you today?

FRED MARTIN

I wouldn't usually come in when I have a runny nose, you know, but the bloody wife thought I best check it out.

DR RACHEL SOLOMON

That's nice of her.

FRED MARTIN

Just fuckin' throwing her weight around! She got plenty of that!

Fred breaks out into a muffled laugh, followed by a cough.

DR RACHEL SOLOMON

Well, from your temperature, it doesn't look like you have got the coronavirus. That's good news.

FRED MARTIN

Fuckin' could have told you that for nothing.

DR RACHEL SOLOMON

I'll take a nasopharyngeal swab and then we'll know for sure. I'd also like to do a blood test if that's alrigh I'll take a fair bet you haven't had one for a while.

FRED MARTIN

I don't bloody care, do I?

Rachel prepares a tray that carries the syringe and three capsules for holding the

blood. She applies a strap to expose a vein and then starts with the extraction.

DR RACHEL SOLOMON
I'll try not to hurt you. Just keep your arm still for me, please.

FRED MARTIN
I know the drill.

DR RACHEL SOLOMON
(giving him a swab test)
This is the real test for the virus.

FRED MARTIN
Go on then.

DR RACHEL SOLOMON
(filling out a form)
Are a smoker?

FRED MARTIN
What do you bloody think? You women are not taking my fuckin' smokes! I'll tell you that for free!

DR RACHEL SOLOMON
How many a day are you smoking then?

FRED MARTIN
I don't fuckin' know! What's it to you anyway?

DR RACHEL SOLOMON
I'm a doctor.

FRED MARTIN
Well fuck me!

DR RACHEL SOLOMON
Just trying to prolong your life.

FRED MARTIN
What fuckin' for? It's a shit life! My fuckin' life anyway! If I want to fuck it then I'll fuck it!

DR RACHEL SOLOMON
As you like.

FRED MARTIN
Damn fuckin' right!

DR RACHEL SOLOMON
Would you like a syrup for your nose and throat?

FRED MARTIN
If you like! I don't fuckin' care. Bloody wife sent me, you see.

DR RACHEL SOLOMON
And you do everything she says?

FRED MARTIN
Fuckin' hell if I don't! You try living with the bitch!

DR RACHEL SOLOMON
So why did you marry her in the first place?

FRED MARTIN
(slowly and introspectively)
Got back from the war and knocked her up.

DR RACHEL SOLOMON
Vietnam?

FRED MARTIN
(nodding)
Fuckin' hell it was. Went in fit and healthy and came out a bloody alcoholic druggie.

DR RACHEL SOLOMON
I've heard it was a bit like that. But you made it through.

FRED MARTIN
I never made it through.

DR RACHEL SOLOMON
What do you mean?

FRED MARTIN
I'm still fuckin' over there.

Rachel looks at Fred with a sort of sad apology. She suspects he's had a tough time since getting back from Vietnam nearly 50 years ago and assumes that the

army hasn't really followed up with him regarding his mental health and addictions.

DR RACHEL SOLOMON
give you a call in a couple of days, once the tests comes back. At your age I would suggest you not go out unless it's absolutely necessary.

FRED MARTIN
(softening up a little)
I know, I've been told before. Thanks Doc.

DR RACHEL SOLOMON
More than welcome Mister Martin. Nice to have met you.

FRED MARTIN
Yeah right. Same here.

Fred leaves the office and Rachel writes a report into her computer.

END OF SCENE 1

2. SCENE 2

INSIDE SAME DOCTOR'S OFFICE FOUR DAYS LATER

Fred goes through the open door and sits stiffly in the chair closest to where Rachel, still masked and gloved, is filling out a report from a previous patient. She looks up and smiles when she sees Fred. The

war images hovering over Fred are still there but a lot dimmer.

DR RACHEL SOLOMON
Ah, Mister Martin. Thank you for coming back in.

FRED MARTIN
That's alright. Nothing else to fuckin' do.

DR RACHEL SOLOMON
Test results came back positive, I'm afraid, and I wanted to discuss with you what your options were.

FRED MARTIN
(not appearing too distressed at the news)
That's nice of you. I was sort of hoping I'd see you again. Enjoyed our last chat.

DR RACHEL SOLOMON
(handing Fred a mask and a set of gloves)
That's nice. So did I. Please put these on so you don't spread the virus any further.

FRED MARTIN
(Fred nods and puts the items on)
First bloody decent sleep, these last couple of days, I've had in fuckin' years.

DR RACHEL SOLOMON
That is good to hear. Why do you think that is?

FRED MARTIN
I've never bloody talked about the war, you see, except with you.

DR RACHEL SOLOMON
I see.

FRED MARTIN
I fuckin' did things over there I'm not proud of.

DR RACHEL SOLOMON
Drugs and drink?

FRED MARTIN
After the first three fuckin' months it was all that kept most of us going. Bloody frightening! I'm still fuckin' frightened by it, if truth be told.

DR RACHEL SOLOMON
've heard that Soldier On is a good organisation that deals with this sort of thing.

FRED MARTIN
I know about them but I couldn't do it.

DR RACHEL SOLOMON
Got to act tough in front of your mates?

FRED MARTIN
(suddenly getting rougher)
Fuckin' right! We beat up the bastards who didn't.

(thinking about what he just said)
I wish I hadn't.

DR RACHEL SOLOMON
War does strange things to people, so I'm told.

FRED MARTIN
Yeah right!

Fred's eyes go a little glazed as he remembers something from those days and shivers a little.

DR RACHEL SOLOMON
Something happened over there didn't it?

FRED MARTIN
(still a bit vacant)
What did you just ask me?

DR RACHEL SOLOMON
There's something you'd like to tell me, isn't there?

FRED MARTIN
(nodding with tears forming in his eyes)
I'm not sure where to begin or how to say it nicely.

DR RACHEL SOLOMON
That's alright. Take your time.

FRED MARTIN
After speaking with you the other day I really felt some of the walls come tumbling down.

DR RACHEL SOLOMON
That's very healthy you know.

FRED MARTIN
I've been keeping the bloody world out for so fuckin' long ...

DR RACHEL SOLOMON
Whatever it is that's troubling you, remember that it was fifty years ago. It really is time to let it go.

FRED MARTIN
I bloody know all that.

DR RACHEL SOLOMON
Conscripted at twenty were you?

FRED MARTIN
(smiling awkwardly)
Only fuckin' lottery I ever won.

DR RACHEL SOLOMON
What were you doing before that?

FRED MARTIN
Trade school. Welding apprentice.

DR RACHEL SOLOMON
Is that what you went into after Vietnam?

FRED MARTIN
Boiler-maker with Blanchards until four years ago. I miss me mates. No one bloody rings me. I stopped trying and there was fuckin' nothing.

DR RACHEL SOLOMON
Blokes can be like that. Friendships of convenience are quite common. Women tend to be able to chat away building long-term relationships while some men find it awkward.

FRED MARTIN
(snapping back into why he was seeing Rachel)
But you wanted to talk about my options with this bloody virus didn't you?

DR RACHEL SOLOMON
I did, but I feel it's more important to get that load you've been carting around off your chest first.

FRED MARTIN
(smiling)
I was hoping to sweep it under the bloody rug again.

DR RACHEL SOLOMON
Not this time.

FRED MARTIN
(taking a deep breath)
Played half forward with Oakleigh, you know. Had a real chance with the VFL. St Kilda had me do a pre-season with them. How was I to fuckin' know it was going to be the highlight of my footy career?

DR RACHEL SOLOMON
You were young.

FRED MARTIN
Me dad came to the intras and they told him I was gonna get a tryout in the twos. Fuckin' called up and that was that.

DR RACHEL SOLOMON
You didn't go back to footy after Vietnam?

FRED MARTIN
(getting a bit angry)
Fuck no! I was real fucked up. Twenty two and fucked.

DR RACHEL SOLOMON
What happened after you did your basic training?

FRED MARTIN
Saigon. After a couple of recon missions it was pretty much Yanks, booze and drugs from then on.

DR RACHEL SOLOMON
Women?

FRED MARTIN
(looking a bit teary)
Not us. There was a ban for the Aussies with all the VC everywhere. You never bloody knew who was who! The C.O. was a fuckin' puritan but some guys snuck out. I didn't.

DR RACHEL SOLOMON
Just wanted to do your time and get back to your footy?

FRED MARTIN
Pretty much.

DR RACHEL SOLOMON
What happened?

FRED MARTIN
One fuckin' mission. Eight of us ducked into the bush to track some VC from a little village about five miles from the base.

Fred wipes his eyes with an old handkerchief and then stuffs it into one of his pants pockets.

FRED MARTIN
We had extra dope on us and all of us fuckin' took the lot in one hit. Should a killed us! We were fuckin' high as kites. All the villages looked the same to me. Came across some huts and started firing.

DR RACHEL SOLOMON
Just like that?

FRED MARTIN
(nodding)
Couldn't fuckin' stop. One magazine after another. People screaming! One woman …

Fred stops and stares at Rachel and then breaks into tears.

DR RACHEL SOLOMON
This is good Fred. What did you do to this woman?

FRED MARTIN
Shot her. Oh my fuckin' God! We torched the huts and I …

Fred sobs uncontrollably. Rachel keeps a shocked gaze at him and says nothing.

FRED MARTIN

Her clothes were half ripped off and I fucked her. She was dead! I was fuckin' off my head! I knew she was dead and I fucked her all the same. Two of me mates did the same. We were fuckin' animals!

DR RACHEL SOLOMON

Oh my god Fred. How do you feel now having told me about it?

FRED MARTIN

I know it's good to talk about things but shit, I still see her face all the time, you know. Last couple of nights though she's left me alone. Fuckin' still don't understand why I did it. Do you?

DR RACHEL SOLOMON

I wasn't in your head at the time, Fred, and I'm not a psychiatrist. It's a little out of my league.

FRED MARTIN

I wasn't in my head at the time either. There's a word for what I did isn't there?

DR RACHEL SOLOMON

Necrophilia?

FRED MARTIN

Yeah, that's it. Can five minutes of lunacy sum up a whole person's life?

DR RACHEL SOLOMON

Of course not. It's pretty significant though.

FRED MARTIN

I was fuckin' doped up like a junkie!

DR RACHEL SOLOMON

You didn't do it again, did you?

FRED MARTIN

(slowly)

No I didn't. Spent the past fifty bloody years trying to say sorry.

DR RACHEL SOLOMON

What happened when you got back to the base?

FRED MARTIN

Fuckin' swore a pact to each other never to tell what really happened. We were fuckin' heroes. We all got medals too. Some fuckin' heroes?

Fred looks around the room as if searching for something.

FRED MARTIN
I looked up the assignment order for the mission and tried to find the village we were meant to hit.

DR RACHEL SOLOMON
Did you find it?

FRED MARTIN
Yeah I found it. Fuckin' miles from the one we took out. Just fuckin' wrong from start to finish.

DR RACHEL SOLOMON
Wow! That's quite some story. That's a hell of a lot of baggage to be carrying. Right or wrong, and we know that under normal circumstances, in a sane body and mind, that this is wrong. When you take a cocktail of war, drugs, fear and sexual urges, anything can happen. I'm not judging you, you know. You've already done a good job of that.

FRED MARTIN
(wiping his face)
You're alright! Yeah, should have bloody seen you years ago, I reckon. You're alright!

DR RACHEL SOLOMON
Getting back to the virus. I've organised a bed at St Vincent's Hospital in the city if that's alright with you?

FRED MARTIN
Can't I just be at home?

DR RACHEL SOLOMON
At your age, I'm afraid it would be better to be under some supervision and also to protect your wife and friends from catching anything from you.

FRED MARTIN
(resigned to it)
Fair enough.

DR RACHEL SOLOMON
I'll call for an ambulance now if you like?

FRED MARTIN
Alright. Thanks.

Rachel dials the ambulance and arranges it to pick up Fred.

Fred slouches back in the chair with his hands over his face.

DR RACHEL SOLOMON
...ll be here soon. We were lucky to get a bed at St Vincent's. Seems there ...e still a few vacant ones at the moment. I'm sure it won't be like that in a week or so.

FRED MARTIN
(introspectively)
Real lucky. Thanks Doc … for everything.

DR RACHEL SOLOMON
You are very welcome, Mister Martin.

FRED MARTIN
Me Dad's name. Just call me Fred if you don't mind.

DR RACHEL SOLOMON
Sure Fred. Just sit outside in the waiting room until your ride comes.

Fred smiles at Rachel and goes outside, closing the door after him. Rachel writes a report into her computer.

3. End of scene 2

SCENE 3

4. INSIDE THE SAME DOCTOR'S OFFICE THREE WEEKS LATER

Rachel, masked and gloved, is sitting at her desk typing a report into her computer.

There is a knock on her door.

DR RACHEL SOLOMON
(Calling out)
Come in.

Doreen, Fred's wife, comes into the office and sits down. She has just turned seventy, also gloved and masked. Warmly dressed in a plain skirt, blouse and heavy woollen jacket. She is carrying a big shopping bag.

DR RACHEL SOLOMON
(reading from a patient card)
Hello, I'm Doctor Solomon, you must be Doreen Martin. How can I help you today?

DOREEN MARTIN
The results of my coronavirus test, please?

DR RACHEL SOLOMON
(checking the computer)
I see that you've had four tests in the past three weeks. All negative, thankfully.

DOREEN MARTIN
That's right.

DR RACHEL SOLOMON
Someone close to you had the virus?

DOREEN MARTIN
My husband.

DR RACHEL SOLOMON
I see. Did he fully recover from it?

DOREEN MARTIN
Yes he did, however …

DR RACHEL SOLOMON

Are you Fred Martin's wife by any chance?

DOREEN MARTIN

You met Fred a few weeks back, didn't you?

DR RACHEL SOLOMON

Oh yes. We had quite a chat too. How is he?

DOREEN MARTIN
(looking a little shocked)

Didn't anybody tell you?

DR RACHEL SOLOMON

Tell me what?

DOREEN MARTIN
(calmly and sadly)

When Fred was given the all clear from St Vincent's he took an overdose and killed himself.

DR RACHEL SOLOMON
(disturbed by the news)

Oh my god!

DOREEN MARTIN

I wanted to see you because Fred was a much changed man after you saw him.

DR RACHEL SOLOMON

We spoke about the war in Vietnam.

DOREEN MARTIN

He told me that too. It was like he had finally come to terms with the horror he must have gone through.

DR RACHEL SOLOMON

He was another war casualty, but I'm sure the army won't see it like that.

DOREEN MARTIN

That would be right. He was a hero too.

DR RACHEL SOLOMON

He told me of the constant fear he was experiencing and that he relived it all nearly every night.

DOREEN MARTIN

Well, to tell you all that is so not like the Fred I knew and married.

DR RACHEL SOLOMON
You must have seen it though.

DOREEN MARTIN
Yes, every night. That is until he saw you that first time. I thought he was dead in the bed that first night he was that peaceful.

DR RACHEL SOLOMON
He told me.

DOREEN MARTIN
I wished he had seen you, or someone like you, a lot earlier too.

DR RACHEL SOLOMON
He said the same thing to me too.

DOREEN MARTIN
(amazed)
Did he really?

DR RACHEL SOLOMON
Oh yes.

Doreen reaches into her shopping bag and takes out a black box with an envelope sticky-taped over it. The letter has "DR SOLOMON" clearly written on it. She hands the box to Rachel.

DOREEN MARTIN
Fred's last wish was for me to give this to you personally. He said you'd understand. Do you?

DR RACHEL SOLOMON
I think I do. Did Fred leave any letter for you as well?

DOREEN MARTIN
Actually he left one each for our kids and one for me.

DR RACHEL SOLOMON
Have you read yours as yet?

DOREEN MARTIN
He apologized to me for all the pain he believed he caused me and asked for some forgiveness. He also instructed me to deliver the box to you.

DR RACHEL SOLOMON
(laughing)
Welcome aboard.

TERRY
is something we can do together and it could be sort of fun and a distraction during this period.

DR RACHEL SOLOMON
I believe Fred wanted me to do it.

TERRY
I'll be in the background then as a backup should you need something.

DR RACHEL SOLOMON
hat would be wonderful. Canberra War Memorial should be first cab off the rank.

TERRY
Ok, let me know how you go while I clean the house again.

Rachel smiles warmly over at Terry, who leaves her bedroom. She retrieves her mobile phone. First she searches the web on her laptop and finds a number for the CWM. She dials it.

Split stage, lighting appears to give life to this effect, with Rachel in bed on one side and a phone ringing in an office on the other.

DR RACHEL SOLOMON
(getting a bit impatient)
Come on! Answer the bloody thing will you?

CAPTAIN MARK WILLIS
Captain Willis.

DR RACHEL SOLOMON
Hi. I thought it would never answer.

CAPTAIN MARK WILLIS
We are on a skeleton staff of three here. The memorial is closed, you know.

DR RACHEL SOLOMON
I thought that might be the case. You might still be able to help me though.

CAPTAIN MARK WILLIS
Who are you? What exactly do you want?

DR RACHEL SOLOMON
Oh sorry, Doctor Rachel Solomon, from Melbourne.

CAPTAIN MARK WILLIS
How can I help?

DR RACHEL SOLOMON
One of my ex patients, Fred Martin, was in a platoon during The Vietnam War
...

CAPTAIN MARK WILLIS
Are you kidding me? Fifty years ago?

DR RACHEL SOLOMON
That's right. The eight members each received the Republic of Vietnam Cross of Gallantry with Palm Unit Citation. Was that a common medal?

CAPTAIN MARK WILLIS
Not really. From memory, about twenty five were awarded during the conflict. All eight got it, you say?

DR RACHEL SOLOMON
That's what Fred said.

CAPTAIN MARK WILLIS
Hold on, I'll look it up on the computer.

DR RACHEL SOLOMON
Thanks.

Willis types away on his PC and soon has a list of the citation winners on his screen.

CAPTAIN MARK WILLIS

Frederick Martin? Part of a search and destroy unit that on the fifteenth of August, 1969, took out the village of Cawait where the VC were mounting attacks on our base. Heavy fighting, platoon outnumbered but completed the task until the village was destroyed. All members returned safe.

DR RACHEL SOLOMON

That must be the one then.

CAPTAIN MARK WILLIS

What about it?

DR RACHEL SOLOMON

Fred told me, before he died, that it wasn't Cawait they hit, but some other village.

CAPTAIN MARK WILLIS
(still clicking keys on his computer)

How did Fred die, by the way?

DR RACHEL SOLOMON

Overdose. Why do you ask?

CAPTAIN MARK WILLIS

That makes four dead by suicide, two by car accidents and one died on the bloody cruise ship in South America from this bloody virus.

DR RACHEL SOLOMON

Wow! Only one left then?

CAPTAIN MARK WILLIS

It was fifty years ago. What's your point anyway?

DR RACHEL SOLOMON

Fred asked me to find the village and apologise.

CAPTAIN MARK WILLIS
(laughing)

That all?

DR RACHEL SOLOMON

Do you have a contact for the last man standing?

CAPTAIN MARK WILLIS

I have an address and phone number but am not allowed to hand it out, you understand. I'll make some enquiry and ask him to contact you if he wants to. It's the best I can do without a court order.

DR RACHEL SOLOMON
Thank you sir, I'll email you my details. Much appreciated.

CAPTAIN MARK WILLIS
Give me something to do. As quiet as a graveyard round here.

DR RACHEL SOLOMON
Here too.

The line clicked off and the split stage disappears. Rachel finds the general contact page for the CWM and sends her details to Captain Willis.

DR RACHEL SOLOMON
(calling out to Terry)
Canberra's on the job!

TERRY
(calling from the other room)
Great start babe!

Rachel begins another search on her phone and dials the Vietnamese embassy in Melbourne.

RECEPTIONIST
(off screen)
Embassy! How can I redirect you?

DR RACHEL SOLOMON
I'm trying to research villages in Vietnam that were destroyed in 1969 during the war. Can you assist?

RECEPTIONIST
(off screen)
We don't have the staff for that sort of enquiry. My advice would be to ring the government office in Hanoi. Do you have the number?

DR RACHEL SOLOMON
The one on your website?

RECEPTIONIST
(off screen)
That's correct. Good luck.

The line clicks off. Rachel dials the number of The Vietnamese Government Offices in Hanoi.

RECEPTIONIST
(off screen)
Lễ tân!

DR RACHEL SOLOMON
Hello, do you speak English?

RECEPTIONIST
(off screen very slowly)
A little. How I help you?

DR RACHEL SOLOMON
Attacks on villages during the war.

RECEPTIONIST
(off screen)
Short staff. Maybe someone know.

DR RACHEL SOLOMON
Thank you.

RECEPTIONIST
(off screen)
Putting through now.

MAJOR Ng LI
(split stage ... Major Li sitting at a desk)
Hello? Major Ng Li.

DR RACHEL SOLOMON
Do you speak English?

MAJOR Ng LI
Yes. I am a translator. You are Australian?

DR RACHEL SOLOMON
Why yes. I'm trying to find a village that was hit by our forces on the fifteenth of August, 1969.

MAJOR Ng LI
Very precise date. Where abouts? I can search our records here. What is this all about anyway, if I can ask?

DR RACHEL SOLOMON
Our records here mention a village of **Cawait near old Saigon.**

MAJOR Ng LI
(typing on his computer)
Cawait was hit on the third of March, 1970, by our forces and again on the second of June, 1971.

DR RACHEL SOLOMON
I see. Any attacks on villages nearby on the fifteenth of August, 1969?

MAJOR Ng LI
(typing on his computer, sounding a bit surprised)
We don't usually have any accurate data about villages back then. But in this case a survivor wrote a note at the time and handed it into our forces when the Americans finally left. There was an attack on the village of Karang. A farming village. Twenty four people killed and seven wounded. You know something about this?

DR RACHEL SOLOMON
I think I do.

MAJOR Ng LI
Very unusual too.

DR RACHEL SOLOMON
How so?

MAJOR Ng LI
Nothing military there and at that time totally supportive of our opposition. Probably helped in changing their opinion, wouldn't you say?

The Major chuckles into the phone.

DR RACHEL SOLOMON
I guess it would have.

MAJOR Ng LI
They did not assist us that much but were of little use to the Americans. Just farmers. What do you know about it, for our records?

DR RACHEL SOLOMON
From what I have been told by a soldier who was there, it was a big mistake. They got the location wrong and started firing.

MAJOR Ng LI
I would imagine that drugs and alcohol were factors too, yes?

DR RACHEL SOLOMON
I think so.

MAJOR Ng LI
Mmm. It was a long time ago.

DR RACHEL SOLOMON
Yes it was.

MAJOR Ng LI
What did you have in mind to do about it?

DR RACHEL SOLOMON
Talk to the town council and maybe offer some financial assistance to make their lives a little better.

MAJOR Ng LI
Good idea. Look up on Google and you'll find some contacts there. It's the best I can suggest.

DR RACHEL SOLOMON
Thank you Major. I will.

MAJOR Ng LI
Good luck.

The phone cuts out and the split stage disappears. Rachel sits up in her bed and writes some notes of her conversation. Her phone rings and she answers. Split stage re-emerges with Brendan, an old weather beaten, unshaved man sitting on his porch outside. Similar images of Vietnam to that of Fred's hover over his head.

DR RACHEL SOLOMON
Rachel.

BRENDAN McCULLOUGH
Are you the friend of Fred's? Fred Martin.

DR RACHEL SOLOMON
I was Fred's doctor, who is this?

BRENDAN McCULLOUGH
BRENDAN McCULLOUGH, we served together in Nam. I got a call to contact you. How is Fred?

DR RACHEL SOLOMON
Thanks for getting back to me Brendan. Fred died a couple of weeks ago, I'm afraid.

BRENDAN McCULLOUGH
Shit! How did he die?

DR RACHEL SOLOMON
Overdose.

BRENDAN McCULLOUGH
Seems to be the fuckin' way for all the unit.

DR RACHEL SOLOMON
I understand that two of your group died in traffic accidents and one from the coronavirus.

BRENDAN McCULLOUGH
(laughing)
Fuckin' traffic accidents! I wouldn't call driving off a bridge a fuckin' accident! I wouldn't call driving into a fuckin' brick wall a fuckin' accident either!

DR RACHEL SOLOMON
I didn't know those details.

BRENDAN McCULLOUGH
Of course you fuckin' wouldn't!

DR RACHEL SOLOMON
Fred told me what really happened on the raid that resulted in your medal.

BRENDAN McCULLOUGH
Fuckin' ancient history.

DR RACHEL SOLOMON
He left some money for me to do something for survivors of that village and I'm in the process of finding them.

BRENDAN McCULLOUGH

Lot of fuckin' good now!

DR RACHEL SOLOMON

It won't help those who are already dead, but it might bring some comfort to those left behind. Including you.

BRENDAN McCULLOUGH
(breaking into a sob)

I've had to live with the bloody thing all my fuckin' life, haven't I?

DR RACHEL SOLOMON

I'm sorry for all of that Brendan. Have you tried the organization "Open Arms"? I believe they offer real help to ex-servicemen like you.

BRENDAN McCULLOUGH

Yeah right! I'm too fuckin' ashamed to tell my story anyway. Fuckin' amazing that Fred did.

DR RACHEL SOLOMON

He was looking for some redemption.

There is a pause on the line as Brendan gathers his thoughts.

BRENDAN McCULLOUGH

Are you looking for money?

DR RACHEL SOLOMON
(alarmed)

Oh, my word, no!

BRENDAN McCULLOUGH
(quiet and thoughtful)

I'd like to give some money, you see.

DR RACHEL SOLOMON

When I find out more details of what is possible, I'll let you know, if you like? I have your number now on my phone.

BRENDAN McCULLOUGH
(relieved)

I would. Thankyou.

DR RACHEL SOLOMON

You are very welcome Brendan. You can call me to talk whenever you like, you know.

Rachel dials the number of the Post Office there and waits for it to be answered. Suddenly it is and there is a split stage again with a woman, Linh Hoang, behind a desk sorting some letters and packages.

LINH HOANG
(Speaking in Vietnamese)
Xin Chao (Sin chow)

DR RACHEL SOLOMON
Do you speak English?

LINH HOANG
Little. What you want?

DR RACHEL SOLOMON
(speaking slowly)
I am from Australia and would like to speak with someone in Karang who speaks good English. Can you direct me?

LINH HOANG
Farmers here. No English. My name is Linh Hoang. What you want?

DR RACHEL SOLOMON
To donate some money to your village.

LINH HOANG
(confused)
What?

DR RACHEL SOLOMON
Can I email you?

LINH HOANG
(confused)
Email? Oh yes, l l n h h o a n g at Hotmail dot com.

DR RACHEL SOLOMON
Ok, thanks.

BRENDAN McCULLOUGH
Thanks. Fuckin' pigs we were.

DR RACHEL SOLOMON
I've never been to war so I don't judge anyone. I just want to help.

BRENDAN McCULLOUGH
Thought I'd get the fuckin' virus and that would be that. But I didn't!

DR RACHEL SOLOMON
I unfortunately did. But it's given me some time to complete Fred's request.

BRENDAN McCULLOUGH
Hope you recover quickly. Should have been me.

The phone line goes dead and the split stage disappears leaving Rachel sitting in her bed jotting Brendan's phone number down in her book of notes.

DR RACHEL SOLOMON
(calling out to Terry)
Might get a bit of a phone bill over this but I feel it will be worth the effort.

TERRY
(calling back)
Sounds like you're making some progress then.

DR RACHEL SOLOMON
I think I am.

TERRY
Great!

Rachel scours her laptop for the village of Karang and is quite excited when she finds it.

DR RACHEL SOLOMON
You beauty!

DR RACHEL SOLOMON

quite sure at the moment but if I can get him to come to terms with the past and let it go, he might have a chance.

TERRY

Suggest therapy. You're not a psychiatrist, you know?

DR RACHEL SOLOMON

My very words. Not that easy to handball this one I'm afraid.

TERRY

Do your best then, hon.

Terry wanders off stage and Rachel composes an email to Linh. She reads it out.

DR RACHEL SOLOMON

Dear Linh, nice to talk to you today, I would like to communicate with the head person of your village relating to a donation from an Australian soldier that the money be used to make life easier and better for you all. Sincerely, Dr Rachel Solomon.

TERRY
(listening from the other room)

Sounds good, Honey. Get Google to translate it into Vietnamese and email both versions to her.

DR RACHEL SOLOMON
(calling back to him)

Good idea, thanks.

Rachel makes the translation from Google and emails the letter. She then re-reads Fred's letter and puts a call into the lawyer, Harry Johns.

Split stage appears again with Harry, in his late sixties, glued to his computer working

on tax statements. He answers the phone reluctantly.

HARRY JOHNS
(bruskly)
Yellow!

DR RACHEL SOLOMON
Harry Johns the lawyer?

HARRY JOHNS
(laughing)
I've been called other things. What can I do you for?

DR RACHEL SOLOMON
Rachel Solomon …

HARRY JOHNS
Ah, Fred Martin's doctor! Am I right?

DR RACHEL SOLOMON
That's right. Just wondering if Fred's will had been cleared as yet?

HARRY JOHNS
Had the OK from the coroner last week, as a matter of fact, did you get my letter?

DR RACHEL SOLOMON
Actually no. I'm at home, isolating, with this virus.

HARRY JOHNS
Sorry to hear that. Was going to call you in a day or so. Fred left an amount of eleven thousand, five hundred and forty two dollars in a trust account to be handed over to you. He said you'd know what to do with it.

DR RACHEL SOLOMON
Eleven Thousand?

HARRY JOHNS
Yep! And a bit of change. Every month or so for the past twenty years he'd get me to put a bit in. What's it for? If I can ask?

DR RACHEL SOLOMON
A donation to a village in Vietnam that he instructed me to arrange.

HARRY JOHNS
I see.

DR RACHEL SOLOMON
Can you handle the final handing over of the money, and is it possible to add any more to it?

HARRY JOHNS
Yes, I can do all that. When you have the details of bank transfer I will handle it gladly. Very nice thing too.

DR RACHEL SOLOMON
I'll email you the details when I know as well as the other donation as well. Will there be an extra charge for doing all of this?

HARRY JOHNS
Thankyou, but it will be my pleasure and privilege to handle this personally and free of charge too.

DR RACHEL SOLOMON
That's very generous of you sir.

HARRY JOHNS
Not at all. It was a dirty war and we shouldn't have been there in the first place. Fred told me a little of what he went through. I'm assuming he told you a lot more. I don't need to know the details but he was a much troubled man. Thank you for calling too.

DR RACHEL SOLOMON
Thank you too. I'll be in touch. Goodbye.

The line ends and the split stage disappears. Rachel hits the redial on her mobile phone and calls Brendan. Split stage reappears.

BRENDAN McCULLOUGH
Hi Doc, that was quick!

DR RACHEL SOLOMON
How are you Brendan.

BRENDAN McCULLOUGH
Surviving.

DR RACHEL SOLOMON
I'm a bit worried about you, actually.

BRENDAN McCULLOUGH
I'm alright.

DR RACHEL SOLOMON
I just spoke with Fred's lawyer, Harry Johns, and if you would like to add anything to Fred's Vietnamese Trust, now is the time to do it.

BRENDAN McCULLOUGH
Yeah, thanks. Text me his details and I'll get on to it.

DR RACHEL SOLOMON
That's great.

BRENDAN McCULLOUGH
Thanks Doc, Just what I bloody needed.

Rachel hears the front door bell ring and a man speak to Terry

ROUGH MAN
(off stage)
Woollies delivery, my man.

TERRY
(off stage)
Didn't think we had a delivery coming.

ROUGH MAN
(off stage)
Somebody did. It's all paid for just sign here.

TERRY
(off stage)
Ok, must have been Rachel.

As Rachel hears Terry open the door she pauses in her conversation with Brendan. Suddenly she hears Terry scream out as he his whacked by a baseball bat and three

hooded men storm into the house and one goes to where Rachel is in bed. Rachel puts her phone under a sheet as she screams out.

DR RACHEL SOLOMON
(screaming)
What's going on! Terry! Terry!

ROUGH MAN
He can't help yous now, bitch!

DR RACHEL SOLOMON
(screaming)
Help! Somebody help me!

ROUGH MAN
Scream all yous like, bitch! No-one will hear yous.

DR RACHEL SOLOMON
(screaming)
Brendan call the police! Brendan!

The Rough Man just laughs as he rips the sheets off Rachel. He notices the mobile phone and grabs it.

ROUGH MAN
Ya won't need this anymore will ya.

DR RACHEL SOLOMON
(screaming)
Listen, I'm a doctor! I've got Covid 19 too! You better keep your distance!

ROUGH MAN
Fuckin' virus is the best thing to happen for a long time.

DR RACHEL SOLOMON
(screaming)
I've got the virus I'm telling you!

ROUGH MAN
I don't fuckin' care is what I'm telling yous!

DR RACHEL SOLOMON
(screaming)
What do you want?

ROUGH MAN
Everything you got, bitch!

DR RACHEL SOLOMON
(screaming)
Oh my God!

The Rough Man rips away at Rachel's bedclothes exposing her nakedness and then punches her in the face. Blood oozes from her nose and mouth as he jumps on top of her and rapes her. She passes out.

Stage gradually darkens.

6. SCENE 5 ... BEDROOM OF RACHEL SOLOMON ... TWO HOURS LATER

Rachel is just coming to her senses as she sees a masked man standing over her. She tries to throw a punch at him but he just catches her fist. As her eyes gain more focus she realizes that he is a police

officer and that a woman police officer, also masked, is standing right next to him.

DR RACHEL SOLOMON
(in a daze)
I've got the virus ...

SERGEANT VLAD ROCCIC
(softly)
I know. I've got an ambulance coming. You'll be alright now.

DR RACHEL SOLOMON
(in a daze)
Where's Terry? Is he alright?

The police lady starts to rearrange Rachel's clothes and helps her to sit up in straight in the bed.

OFFICER JESSIE WATKINS
There's a medical officer looking at him now. Do you remember anything?

DR RACHEL SOLOMON
(in a daze)
A hooded man ...

Rachel suddenly realizes what has happened to her and she breaks into a sob.

DR RACHEL SOLOMON
I was raped. Oh my God! How did you know?

OFFICER JESSIE WATKINS
A Brendan McCullough from Queensland phoned it through to us and we responded as quickly as we could. He didn't have your address so there was some time delay, I'm sorry.

DR RACHEL SOLOMON
Brendan ...

OFFICER JESSIE WATKINS
Friend of yours?

DR RACHEL SOLOMON
No. Just someone I was talking with.

OFFICER JESSIE WATKINS
Lucky for you he was on the ball. Ex-army I would say by the way he reported it in.

DR RACHEL SOLOMON
Vietnam …

OFFICER JESSIE WATKINS
Yeah, that figures.

DR RACHEL SOLOMON
My mobile and laptop …

OFFICER JESSIE WATKINS
We found some items like that outside. Your fridge and pantry have been trashed. Food raiding with violence is becoming a bit common.

DR RACHEL SOLOMON
Vietnam War medals?

OFFICER JESSIE WATKINS
No, not yet. Let me know exact details of them and we'll keep a lookout.

DR RACHEL SOLOMON
Sure … Thanks.

OFFICER JESSIE WATKINS
Take it easy and we'll speak to you again in a couple of days. Ok?

Rachel nods her head, tears still dripping from her eyes as two ambulance officers come into the room and put Rachel onto a stretcher and wheel her out as the stage darkens again.

7. SCENE 6 RACHEL'S OFFICE FOUR WEEKS LATER

Rachel makes her way into her old office and settles in behind her desk. She turns on her computer. Her mobile phone rings and she sees it is from overseas so she answers it.

DR RACHEL SOLOMON
Rachel.

A split stage again sees an old man and a young girl sitting at a family kitchen table. They are both Vietnamese. Nguyen Van Lu and his granddaughter Nguyen Phuong.

NGUYEN PHUONG
Are you the lady who sent the email a month ago?

DR RACHEL SOLOMON
(terror appearing on Rachel's face as she remembers what happened after she sent the email)
Yes, it was me. Doctor Rachel Solomon, who are you?

NGUYEN PHUONG
Nguyen Phuong. I am with my grandfather Nguyen van Lu. He wants to know if this is about what happened in his village during the war.

DR RACHEL SOLOMON
(becoming fully awake)
Yes it is.

Rachel hears Phuong talking to her grandfather in Vietnamese.

NGUYEN PHUONG
He orders me to tell you that he doesn't want any of the money. That it's blood-money. He was there on the day when Australian soldiers came into his village and started killing our people.

DR RACHEL SOLOMON
I'm so sorry …

NGUYEN PHUONG
His first wife was killed and raped. Many others killed and wounded.

DR RACHEL SOLOMON
I'm so sorry. I've only just learnt of what went on. Terrible! Simply terrible!

NGUYEN PHUONG
Long time ago. No reminding him, please.

DR RACHEL SOLOMON
Of course. Can you think of anything I can do with this money that is left to me?

NGUYEN PHUONG
(laughing)
We need a hospital and doctors like you.

DR RACHEL SOLOMON
I don't think there's enough for that to happen, but I'll bare it in mind. Keep well and safe from the virus.

NGUYEN PHUONG
Thank you for contacting us. No virus here in this village. Goodbye.

DR RACHEL SOLOMON
Goodbye. Lucky you.

The split stage disappears leaving Rachel alone in her office staring at her computer screen. Her phone rings.

DR RACHEL SOLOMON
Rachel.

OFFICER JESSIE WATKINS
(off screen/stage)
Jessie Watkins, Victoria Police. How are you doing?

DR RACHEL SOLOMON
Oh yes. Not too bad thankyou.

OFFICER JESSIE WATKINS
(off screen/stage)
Just letting you know that we caught the three offenders and they are due to face court on Wednesday.

DR RACHEL SOLOMON
(a shocked look on her face)
Do I need to do anything?

OFFICER JESSIE WATKINS
(off screen/stage)
Not if you don't want to. It would be virtually impossible for you to identify the man who raped you and we have enough forensic evidence from you to DNA from him to more than cover it. I'll let you know though.

DR RACHEL SOLOMON
Thank you. By the way, how did you find them?

OFFICER JESSIE WATKINS
(off screen/stage)
Vietnam War medals. Not too many like them. It wasn't that hard to trace them back to those men.

DR RACHEL SOLOMON
(thoughtfully and sadly)
Why is it always men?

OFFICER JESSIE WATKINS
(off screen/stage)
Nature of the beast, I'm afraid.

DR RACHEL SOLOMON
Nature of men, more like it.

The line clicks off and Rachel gets a knock on her door.

DR RACHEL SOLOMON
Come in.

DOREEN MARTIN
Hello doctor. Do you remember me?

DR RACHEL SOLOMON
Mrs. Martin. How are you?

DOREEN MARTIN
I'm alright. I heard what happened to you and was concerned.

DR RACHEL SOLOMON
That's very nice of you. It will take some time for me, that's for sure, but my plan is to dust myself off and get back into my work. Best medicine I think.

DOREEN MARTIN
I'm sure you know what's best.

DR RACHEL SOLOMON
Can I do anything for you today?

DOREEN MARTIN
I'm fine thanks. I wondered if you could tell me what Fred confided in you and why he left a sum of money in your care.

DR RACHEL SOLOMON
Fred was a very troubled man since his service in the army, as you well know. He felt that he would like to donate some money to the people of Vietnam.

DOREEN MARTIN
I see.

DR RACHEL SOLOMON
Not that they want it from him.

DOREEN MARTIN
Really? What happens to it now, then?

DR RACHEL SOLOMON
Not sure. I'll work something out.

DOREEN MARTIN
Fair enough.

DR RACHEL SOLOMON
That's not what you came to see me about isn't it?

DOREEN MARTIN
Aha!

DR RACHEL SOLOMON
Is there something you'd like to tell me?

DOREEN MARTIN
(looking very serious)
Would you say that Fred could have been a rapist?

DR RACHEL SOLOMON
Why would you ask that?

DOREEN MARTIN
What did he write in his letter to you, then?

DR RACHEL SOLOMON
Only that he appreciated chatting with me and that he wanted me to handle some donation for him.

DOREEN MARTIN
When you spoke with Fred, did he mention anything about rape?

DR RACHEL SOLOMON
You know I'm not at liberty to discuss confidential discussions with anyone.

DOREEN MARTIN
For Christ's sake, he's dead and gone!

DR RACHEL SOLOMON
What's this all about anyway?

DOREEN MARTIN
It's true then, isn't it? I can tell on your face anyway.

DR RACHEL SOLOMON
We talked about the war in Vietnam is all.

DOREEN MARTIN
My daughter came to see me two weeks ago while you were away. She showed me Fred's letter to her where he apologized for not being a better father to her.

DR RACHEL SOLOMON
And?

DOREEN MARTIN
She then told me that he raped her for nearly three years, starting when she was ten years old. Can you believe that?

DR RACHEL SOLOMON
(looking horrified)
No I can't!

DOREEN MARTIN
Well neither could I, at first. I mean, I would have known wouldn't I?

DR RACHEL SOLOMON
One would think so.

DOREEN MARTIN
She told me that for years now she has been in therapy and that she even tried to kill herself. She gave me the name of the psychiatrist to prove it all.

DR RACHEL SOLOMON
Did you contact the doctor?

DOREEN MARTIN
I did. It all happened under my very nose and I didn't know anything! Honestly!

DR RACHEL SOLOMON
Does your daughter blame you, or something like that?

DOREEN MARTIN
(nodding with tears forming in her eyes)
I had no idea! Men!

DR RACHEL SOLOMON
(trying to comfort her)
It's not all men.

DOREEN MARTIN
Yeah, but it's always men, isn't it?

DR RACHEL SOLOMON
I guess that's true enough.

DOREEN MARTIN
My daughter believes that I let her down, and in some way I did. It's so hard to deal with something that I didn't know about and that happened a long time ago.

DR RACHEL SOLOMON
Is she still going for counselling sessions?

DOREEN MARTIN
She is. Probably one of the reasons her own marriage broke down.

DR RACHEL SOLOMON
These things are time bombs and manifest themselves in all sorts of ways.

DOREEN MARTIN
I suppose you're not going to divulge exactly what Fred said to you are you?

DR RACHEL SOLOMON
In my opinion, it would really serve no benefit to you, believe me. Let's just say that he was a troubled man who finally laid to rest his demons in the only way he knew how.

DOREEN MARTIN

And now I have to deal with the guilt of it.

DR RACHEL SOLOMON

You must be the judge as to how harsh you are on yourself. You may be criticized for being blind, but your love for your family was very constant throughout.

DOREEN MARTIN

It's like I've lost touch with my family through this. My son said some nasty things to me. Words spoken cannot be unsaid.

DR RACHEL SOLOMON

That is true. But I feel that time is the greatest healer of all things. And in time, you would hope he and your daughter will find a way to forgive you and themselves for the harshness of what their father caused you all.

DOREEN MARTIN

We will see, won't we?

DR RACHEL SOLOMON

How else can we live wholesomely if not through some form of forgiveness?

DOREEN MARTIN
(getting up to leave)
If you ever change your mind.

DR RACHEL SOLOMON

The Hippocratic Oath.

DOREEN MARTIN

Here we go again. Men protecting men.

(under her breath)
Hiding the truth once more.

The End

THE COFFIN

by

Peter Levy

Copyright 2020

1. Int. Funeral Parlor

Stephen Bryant, 45, *is lying in the coffin and suddenly rises up to face the audience to chat about his life and demise.*

Nancy *is his wife*

Ray *was his* best friend

Julie *was his lover, she is now pregnant*

Stephen, Julie & Ray *worked together for ASIO*

They take turns in visiting him and having their say.

He comments after they each leave

The three people chat between themselves

He sums it all up

STEPHEN
(rising from the coffin looking confused)
What the fuck!
Where am I?

(Realizing his situation)
Oh yeah. I was shot.
Shit! I'm dead!

(directly to the audience)
I guess you're wondering what that feels like. Right?
Well, it doesn't feel at all.
Not physically or emotionally.
Nothing!

I had this coming. I guess in some way, we all have to face this moment sooner or later.

(he chuckles)
Later, rather than sooner.

Stephen looks around the funeral parlour and then at the audience.

I wasn't the nicest guy around or the best father. Certainly not the best husband. In my line of work I was too exposed to all sorts of women living on the edge, so to speak, looking for light diversions of the sexual nature. I sure didn't oppose such views. It was what it was. Didn't mean that much, really. I loved my wife, you see.

I worked in counter espionage in a department of ASIO. Sounds pretty cool and James Bondish doesn't it? Pretty boring most of the time, actually. Part of my job description was to stir up the pot against China, Iran, Muslims, Jews, Blacks, White Supremists, Covid 19, climate change. You name it, we had an opinion about it.

It was all about governmental control and how to keep it. Not rocket science. Engendering fear of a perceived threat was my speciality and I was very good at it.

It helps when you don't believe in anything.

Fresh out of uni I was the right man for the job. A cynic who only cared about how much reaction I could get from my nonsense and how much money I could earn or glean from the system.

We had scams upon scams working in the background that at times made it damn hard to remember what was real or "truthful", when it flared up within some article in a newspaper.

That a lot of my fantasies were given a life was quite amazing.

The real stuff did pop up every now and again and was relatively kids play to handle, after the games and simulation exercises we were doing all the time.

But not always.

In my department I was also directly involved in a joint countries covert activity called Nitro Zoos. It used to be called Ducks Nest and before that it was Olympic Games. Probably called something else now. It was state of the art coordinated cyber warfare aimed at Iran and involving us, The USA, Israel, Great Britain, France and Germany. To summarize what we were doing, in laymen terms, was to simply put as many roadblocks as we could in the way of the Iranian nuclear reactors so that their full potential of weapon use would never be realized.

Started out so gung-ho and the software was mind-boggling. Encryptions so deep and sleeping, that the Iranians had no idea why their plants were malfunctioning and blowing up. No idea why key people and scientists were dying or defecting.

But, and there's always a but, the whole scene was turned on its head when the Russians found out what we were doing, cracked the coding of our software with Pakistani cyber experts and then used the same technology and software, with appropriate changes, right back against us all. It was war. Still going on too.

It didn't worry me one way or the other. That is until last week when I got shot and killed in an exchange with some so-called terrorists in the city mall. You might have read about it. I was a hero for being hit! Ha! Some hero!

My intel take on the event would have been that it wasn't as random as one might have thought. Someone over there saw my name as part of a team that they were targeting and simply put a red line through it and took me out. We were being aggressive and this was a message, loud and clear, that the game rules had changed and to watch out.

We always tried to make small actions that were happening appear a lot bigger, more organized, more dangerous to the public, more connected to wider issues, than we knew they were. They were just random opportunities to justify our tenuous position in the society we were manipulating.

I think in my case it wasn't one of those random opportunities. That's why I say, I had it coming.

Stephen slides back into his coffin as Nancy, his wife, comes in. She is dressed in widow's black. She approaches the coffin and looks inside.

NANCY
(a bit teary and sighing)
Oh Stephen, you've really done it now haven't you?

(Nancy pauses and wipes her eyes and nose)
I always thought that you were making up the terror threats that were out there on the streets so as to not share in the daily housework and general parenting duties. Maybe I was wrong?

Forgive me Stephen! There you were, doing your best to keep us and the rest of the country safe, while I was only thinking of myself.

(Nancy pauses and thinks a little)

You know that Ray has had his eyes on me for quite a while now. I don't know if you knew. Doesn't matter now, of course. He was your best friend and all. I want you to know that I never gave him a second thought. Honestly! Cheating on you might not have meant much to him, as he was quite prepared to cheat on his wife, but I would never have been a part of it. For me, it was always you from the moment we tied the knot.

Anyway, a man who'd cheat on his wife would be no bargain. I'd never be able to trust him, like I trusted you.

But it was nice to know that I still had something that men wanted. Nice to be looked at in that way.

Oh Stephen! Why did this have to happen? You look so peaceful lying there too. Why did this have to happen now?

Nancy looks lovingly into the coffin. Her look changes to fear as she ponders as to what her new life will look like.

I've heard of vagrant opportunistic men prying on lonely widows and then taking them for everything they can get their greasy hands onto. I used to laugh at those stories and never once thought I'd be in that same boat myself. Oh Stephen, what am I supposed to do now then?

Nancy cries a little and wipes her eyes with her handkerchief.
She then stares at the coffin with a stern look.

You have sure left me in a fine mess, haven't you?

Thinking about what she just verbalized she feels guilty.

Oh Stephen, I didn't *mean* that! I didn't mean that!

Nancy leaves the room sobbing. Stephen sits up in the coffin.

STEPHEN

Yeah, it will be a bit of a challenge for her. Nothing I can do about that from here. She was a good wife alright and living with me would not have been easy. I wouldn't blame her if she chose a guy like Ray, but she'd be getting another bloke just like me. I know what he's about. No loyalties to me if he can have a screw of her every so often. I probably would have considered the same if the shoe was on the other foot. He doesn't care that much for Nancy as Nancy, it would be just a case of new sex for the excitement and sake of it. She would probably read into it a whole different picture, I'll bet.

I was playing around too, just like Ray was. Yeah, and it was fun too! He'd probably go after Julie if he could, but I doubt she'd have him. My broken promises of leaving Nancy must still be resonating in her brain and jumping into another relationship with a bloke that is already married would be the last thing she'd want to do. Ray and I were two peas from the same pod.

Ray Harris, medium height and build, a little balding. Best friend to Stephen and they worked in the same building for the same company, but on different departments that handled other issues.

Ray walks into the room and goes straight over to the coffin. He looks inside and then steps back a bit.

RAY
(to Stephen)

Well, well, Steve. I thought you'd look a lot worse with a couple of bullets in you. You don't look so bad, really. Those morticians know their stuff alright. When I first saw you ... let's say, you look a lot better now.

Wow! I really figured that I would have been the first one to get it, not you. Cyber security is not that dangerous an occupation one would have thought. I wonder if you were taken out on purpose or if it was some random act. I don't believe in random and chance. Not in our business anyway. Coincidence is another thing I don't buy. Can't afford to. Don't worry, I'll follow it up and get some revenge happening for you. The least I can do.

Confession time buddy. I've been having these thoughts and dreams about being with Nancy. Hope you don't mind. Nah, you would do the same, wouldn't you? She's a good looking woman for her age, I bet she'd be great in the sack too. I'll keep a watchful eye on her and the kids for you. You would have done the same for me.

I bet I've missed something. I looked over the CTV footage and read the official junk, but there must be something else there. What were you working on? There's got to be a connection. Any guy in our line of work is a target and there's a clue out there. It's just that I can't see it or figure it out as yet. But I will. You know I will too.

See you later Steve.

Ray saunters off out of the room and Stephen rises once more from his coffin.

STEPHEN

Yeah, I'll see you later buddy. I will bloody miss you, I think. We had some great times alright.

don't mind, really, that you want to have a go with Nancy. You were right. I often thought what it would be like to be with your wife too. I guess we are pretty similar in that respect.

About revenge. Well, firstly I don't give a fuck about it. And secondly, you wouldn't have a clue about cyber warfare. That's why we worked in separate departments. Horses for courses. I appreciate the thought though. You are hardwired like that. Got to get to the bottom of things to sign off completely. In this case you'll be floundering from day one. I can't even figure out why they thought I was so important in the scheme of things. We were the small fry, just cogs in the big wheel. The real action is with the Yanks and Israelis. I wonder if they orchestrated the whole thing. Maybe I inadvertently uncovered something that I shouldn't have. But what? I wasn't that important or that good. We were pretty much observers. Certainly not players.

Stephen slides back into his coffin as Julie makes her way into the room. She makes straight for the coffin and stares for a long time at Stephen lying there. She places a red rose and purposely makes sure a large thorn pricks into his skin to see if there was any reaction. To make sure he was really dead.

JULIE

Sorry Stevie, I had to do that. What a shit thing to happen ... for both of us. I saw your wife, Nancy, out there. She's not a bad sort.

Maybe I'm feeling a bit guilty. I don't know.

You're dead and I'm alone. It just won't feel the same when I walk into the office with someone else sitting in your office.

Do you know who did it to you?

More likely the Americans and Israelis cleaning up their mess. You must have seen something you shouldn't have. Bloody shit business! I love it, but it deals in human misery thousands of miles away. I would have left if you hadn't been there. Probably will after all this dies down. If I left now I would definitely be on a list somewhere and this could happen to me.

Oh Stevie …. What about our plans?

You probably were never going to leave Nancy though. I get that. You posed the illusion and I lived in a delusion. I think, deep down, I always knew you were lying to me about all of that. In our business, that's all we are taught to do from day one. So what did I expect? Ha!

I did love you though and I know you loved me too. Even if you could never leave Nancy. You probably loved her too. Men can do that. I don't think I could though.

Julie looks sadly at the coffin again and walks out of the room.

Stephen slides back up with a grin on his dead face.

STEPHEN
That's why we are different, I guess.

(thinking aloud)

Why would you feel guilty after all this time?

I wandered out of the office to get my sandwich at the deli, like I usually do. Yeah! Like I usually do! That's a match! An incident was happening and two bullets happen to hit me. One through my windpipe, so I couldn't suddenly say something that might incriminate somebody, and the next bullet kills me with a direct hit on my temple. Perfect sniper's kill shot.

That's three matches, if I was looking for a coincident or just bad luck. Being in the wrong place at the wrong time.

Nah! There's something more but I sure can't figure it out. There has to be! I reckon Ray and Julie will work it out though. It's in their blood to check all the angles.

What is it I'm missing?

Stephen slides back into the coffin as Ray and Julie come back into the room and look into the coffin once more.

RAY
Looks pretty good for a dead man.

JULIE
What's the stuff on his face do you think?

RAY
Clay. They use it to fill in the holes made by the bullets.

JULIE
Really? I never knew that.

RAY
I've seen it before. One of the tricks of the trade.

JULIE

Did you see him straight after the shooting?

RAY

I did. He was a mess, too.

JULIE

I wonder if he tried to mouth a message at the end.

RAY

Nothing that I picked up on. You know I would have seen it if he had.

JULIE

Yeah I figured that too. There has got to be something we are both missing.

RAY

Maybe so, maybe not.

JULIE

We don't believe in random.

RAY

Yep. I'll take another look into it, of course. He was my best friend.

JULIE

Mine too.

Nancy comes back into the room and goes over to Ray and Julie.

Nancy

I can't believe he's gone.

Ray

He was a great guy.

Nancy

Do you think it was just bad luck or a work thing?

RAY

Not sure. Julie and I will look into it a bit later.

Julie nods gives Nancy's hand a gentle squeeze.

JULIE
We are all going to miss him terribly.

NANCY
(teary)
Thanks to both of you. You were real friends to Stephen.

They look sadly at each other as Nancy leaves the room again.

RAY
(thoughtfully)
There was a strange bit …

JULIE
(looking up very interested)
What do you mean?

RAY
The calibre of the bullets …

JULIE
What about them?

RAY
The ones in the street were regular point three O but the two that hit Steve were point three one O

JULIE
Pretty close though.

RAY
Yeah, but all the reports termed them as point three O

JULIE
What are you saying?

RAY
We usually call anything that close as point three O and assumed it was the guys in the mall doing the shooting.

JULIE
Wouldn't those guys have a few guns on them, just in case?

RAY
I guess so. I still don't like it though.

JULIE
(smiling gently to Ray)
That's you alright.

RAY
I guess so. I have to get back to the office before the funeral starts. See you later.

JULIE
Sure. I'll be here.

Ray leaves the room as Julie sits down in a chair and types a text into her mobile phone.

Stephen slides up in his coffin. Unseen to Julie.

STEPHEN
(thinking)
Different calibres?

I wonder why Julie didn't make more comment about that when Ray mentioned it. I would have.

Stephen looks over at Julie.

I'm sure she has a point three O gun. Never checked the fine detail though. I wonder if there's a connection.

I'm pretty certain we were given the same calibre guns too.

(continuing the thought)

She could have changed the barrel so that the exactness of the markings on the bullet wouldn't match hers. I would have done that if I wanted to avoid suspicion. And using a calibre that was very common would have been a very smart move too. I would have done that too.

Ray will most likely come to the same conclusions as me. We are very alike in many ways.

Am I still missing something? Why do I mistrust Julie so much?

We always had so much fun when we got together.

I know I promised a lot of things to her that I never intended to honour.

Could that be a reason to kill me?

JULIE
(looking over at Stephen and the coffin)
Oh Stevie ... if only you were more honest with me.

I loved you so much.

Look what you made me do.

STEPHEN
(a look of shock on his face)
I knew it! You did do it!

Why?

JULIE
I would have done anything and everything for you. You never intended to leave Nancy didn't you?

Love and hate are very closely related you know.

Julie goes back to her chair and browses her mobile phone.

She sends a couple of texts

Stephen watches her in amazement and disappointment.

STEPHEN
(resignedly)
I never would have picked it.

Ray comes back into the room and heads over to Julie.

She looks up and smiles at him.

JULIE
Find anything?

RAY
If I was looking for an inside job then you would be on the list.

JULIE
Yeah?

RAY
You two were the only ones with point three one O weapons.

JULIE
He didn't kill himself. So now you're looking at me are you?

RAY
(shaking his head)
I know where you were at the time. You're clear.

JULIE
(amazed)
Really? Where was I then?

RAY
Doctor Taylor, in Malvern, getting confirmation of your pregnancy test and that you wanted to go through with it and have the child regardless.

JULIE
(annoyed)
Isn't anything sacred?

RAY
Not in our business. When were you planning to tell Steve?

JULIE
Later that day, actually.

RAY
He was never going to leave Nancy, you know.

JULIE
I'm not that dumb. I did hope that this might change his mind a bit though. I've done it now though.

RAY
Good luck.

Stephen has a shocked expression on his face as he faces Julie.

STEPHEN
You bitch!

But if you didn't kill me ... who did?

RAY
(to Julie)
You wait in the chapel. Ask Nancy to come in for a chat.

JULIE
What are you up to?

RAY
Not sure. Just do it.

JULIE
(leaving the room)
Ok.

STEPHEN
(looking at Ray)
What the fuck are you up to? A bit quick to make a play for her isn't it?

Nancy comes back into the room and stands next to the coffin.

NANCY
(casually)
You wanted to speak to me Ray?

RAY
(looking at Stephen)
When did you find out about Steve and Julie?

STEPHEN
What the fuck?

NANCY
What do you mean?

STEPHEN
Yeah, what do you bloody mean?

RAY
Come on, you must have known I'd figure that much out.

NANCY
About six months ago.

RAY
Your dad was SAS wasn't he? Murdered in his car about four years ago? No witnesses, country road, middle of the day.

NANCY
That's right, he was.

RAY
No bullet casings too. Very professional hit.

NANCY
What are you getting at?

RAY
I don't like similarities without drawing some conclusions.

NANCY
You think the same person killed Stephen?

RAY
What do you think?

NANCY
I wouldn't know.

STEPHEN
What game are playing buddy?

RAY
Your father teach you how to shoot a gun?

NANCY
(shocked)
What?

RAY
I know about the workshop at your parents' house with the targets and firing range.

NANCY
He did actually. I quite enjoyed it too.

RAY
I'll bet! You got real good at it didn't you?

NANCY
So?

RAY

Just a long shot ... but your dad was a bit rough on your mum ... pretty violent at times too, so I'm told. I reckon you killed him to protect her. What do you say to that?

NANCY

Fantasy! Me kill my own dad?

RAY

That's what I think, Nancy.

NANCY

You're crazy! That's what I think!

STEPHEN

Me too!

RAY

I remember going through that case file ad yours were the only clear prints we could find. We totally discounted them, just like you figured we would. A father and daughter would drive around together.

NANCY

If I did it then how would I have got back from the country? He was killed in the middle of nowhere.

RAY

That was the sheer beauty of it. We didn't find the car for a full day.

Steve was probably out of town and you walked and caught a train back. It must have taken you two days I reckon.

I remember we couldn't find you at the time, and when we did, you said you were out shopping.

NANCY

You are a weirdo!

RAY

Your old man had a property that he got rent from that he left to you to handle. Correct?

NANCY

So?

RAY

Very close to our office too.

NANCY

Well?

RAY

I think you must have gone down there one time about six months back to check it out when the tenant left. That's when you happened to see Steve and Julie.

NANCY

Some imagination alright!

RAY

You probably noticed that Steve always went near the building on his way to get his lunch. He was a creature of habit. You waited and then took him out.

NANCY

Where's your proof?

STEPHEN

Yeah, where's your damn proof?

NANCY

Who's going to believe that cock and bull story?

RAY

I don't need proof. I know what happened and that's all there is to it.

NANCY
(alarmed and relieved)

And that's it?

RAY
(smiling)

You were really good. Damn good!

NANCY
(smugly)

So glad you approve.

Stephen slides back into his coffin as Julie comes back into the room and the three of them stare at the coffin in silence.

THE END.

www.ingramcontent.com/pod-product-compliance
Lightning Source LLC
Chambersburg PA
CBHW010244010526
44107CB00061B/2670